Ray, Randolph.
100 great religious
poems.

100 GREAT RELIGIOUS POEMS

100

GREAT RELIGIOUS POEMS

EDITED BY Randolph Ray, RECTOR

THE CHURCH OF THE TRANSFIGURATION

(*The Little Church around the Corner*)

ROYALE HOUSE
MIAMI, FLORIDA

Reprinted 1971

PRINTED IN THE UNITED STATES OF AMERICA

CONTENTS

»» INTRODUCTION ««

TODAY, as never before in my lifetime, people everywhere are seeking reassurance, solace, surcease from fear. And from the Bible, religious poetry, hymns and prayer, they find quietness of mind and in that quietness, strength.

The present collection, covering as it does all kinds of religious verse, is drawn from many sources. No collection of religious poetry would be complete without some examples from that greatest and richest of all anthologies, the Bible. From the Bible I have chosen, among others, the Twenty-third Psalm, the Lord's Prayer, and selections from The Sermon on the Mount. Also included are the great and familiar hymns, the prayers and the best of the sacred poetry penned by the world's most inspired poets of various faiths.

Because I have limited this collection to one hundred poems, it becomes immediately obvious that many favorites will have been omitted. But it is my earnest hope that what is contained here will help the reader in his "twofold yearning to raise earth to Heaven; to draw Heaven down to earth." These poems are limited to no faith, time or age. Wherever man seeks comfort, understanding and an affinity with God—whatever may be his difficulty or pain—however dark or hopeless may appear his future—he will find help in these soul-stirring poems of the ages.

RANDOLPH RAY

February, 1951
New York

100 GREAT RELIGIOUS POEMS

TWENTY-THIRD PSALM

THE LORD is my shepherd; I shall not want.
He maketh me to lie down in green pastures,
He leadeth me beside the still waters.
He restoreth my soul.
He leadeth me in the paths of righteousness for his name's sake.
Yea, though I walk through the valley of the shadow of death,
I will fear no evil: For thou art with me;
Thy rod and thy staff they comfort me.
Thou preparest a table before me in the presence of mine enemies;
Thou anointest my head with oil;
My cup runneth over.
Surely goodness and mercy shall follow me all the days of my life,
And I will dwell in the house of the Lord for ever.

NEARER, MY GOD, TO THEE

Sarah Flower Adams

NEARER, my God, to Thee,
  Nearer to Thee!
E'en though it be a cross
  That raiseth me;
Still all my song shall be,
Nearer, my God, to Thee,
  Nearer to Thee!

Though like the wanderer,
  The sun gone down,
Darkness be over me,
  My rest a stone;
Yet in my dreams I'd be
Nearer, my God, to Thee,
  Nearer to Thee!

There let my way appear
  Steps unto heaven;
All that Thou sendest me
  In mercy given;
Angels to beckon me
Nearer, my God, to Thee,
  Nearer to Thee!

Then, with my waking thoughts
  Bright with Thy praise,

Out of my stony griefs,
  Altars I'll raise;
So by my woes to be
Nearer, my God, to Thee,
  Nearer to Thee!

Or, if on joyful wing,
  Cleaving the sky,
Sun, moon, and stars forgot,
  Upward I fly,
Still all my song shall be
Nearer, my God, to Thee,
  Nearer to Thee!

A HYMN TO GOD THE FATHER

John Donne

WILT THOU forgive that sin where I begun,
  Which was my sin, though it were done before?
Wilt Thou forgive that sin, through which I run,
  And do run still, though still I do deplore?
    When Thou hast done, Thou hast not done,
      For I have more.

Wilt Thou forgive that sin which I have won
  Others to sin, and made my sin their door?
Wilt Thou forgive that sin which I did shun
  A year or two, but wallowed in a score?
    When Thou hast done, Thou hast not done,
      For I have more.

I have a sin of fear, that when I have spun
  My last thread, I shall perish on the shore;
But swear by Thyself, that at my death Thy Son
  Shall shine as he shines now, and heretofore;
    And, having done that, Thou hast done;
      I fear no more.

THE SHEPHERD BOY SINGS

John Bunyan

HE THAT is down needs fear no fall,
He that is low, no pride;
He that is humble ever shall
Have God to be his guide.

I am content with what I have,
Little be it or much;
And, Lord, contentment still I crave,
Because Thou savest such.

Fullness to such a burden is
That go on pilgrimage:
Here little, and hereafter bliss
Is best from age to age.

From THE SERMON ON THE MOUNT

St. Matthew, Chapter 5

BLESSED are the poor in spirit: for theirs is the kingdom of heaven.

Blessed are they that mourn: for they shall be comforted.

Blessed are the meek: for they shall inherit the earth.

Blessed are they which do hunger and thirst after righteousness: for they shall be filled.

Blessed are the merciful: for they shall obtain mercy.

Blessed are the pure in heart: for they shall see God.

Blessed are the peacemakers: for they shall be called the children of God.

Blessed are they which are persecuted for righteousness' sake: for theirs is the kingdom of heaven.

RECESSIONAL

Rudyard Kipling

GOD OF our fathers, known of old,
  Lord of our far-flung battle line,
Beneath whose awful hand we hold
  Dominion over palm and pine:
Lord God of hosts, be with us yet,
Lest we forget, lest we forget.

The tumult and the shouting dies,
  The captains and the kings depart;
Still stands thine ancient sacrifice,
  An humble and a contrite heart:
Lord God of hosts, be with us yet,
Lest we forget, lest we forget.

Far-called our navies melt away,
  On dune and headland sinks the fire;
Lo, all our pomp of yesterday
  Is one with Nineveh and Tyre!
Judge of the Nations, spare us yet,
Lest we forget, lest we forget!

If, drunk with sight of power, we loose
  Wild tongues that have not Thee in awe,
Such boastings as the Gentiles use,
  Or lesser breeds without the law:
Lord God of hosts, be with us yet,
Lest we forget, lest we forget.

For heathen heart that puts her trust
In reeking tube and iron shard;
All valiant dust that builds on dust,
And guarding, calls not Thee to guard.
For frantic boast and foolish word,
Thy mercy on thy people, Lord!

CALVARY

Edwin Arlington Robinson

FRIENDLESS and faint, with martyred steps and slow,
Faint for the flesh, but for the spirit free
Stung by the mob that came to see the show,
The Master toiled along to Calvary;
We jibed him, as he went, with houndish glee,
Till his dimmed eyes for us did overflow;
We cursed his vengeless hands thrice wretchedly,—
And this was nineteen hundred years ago.

But after nineteen hundred years the shame
Still clings, and we have not made good the loss
That outraged faith has entered in his name.
Ah, when shall come love's courage to be strong!
Tell me, O Lord—tell me, O Lord, how long
Are we to keep Christ writhing on the cross!

THE LORD'S PRAYER

St. Matthew, Chapter 6

Our Father which art in heaven,
Hallowed be thy name.
Thy kingdom come.
Thy will be done in earth, as it is in heaven.
Give us this day our daily bread.
And forgive us our debts, as we forgive our debtors.
And lead us not into temptation, but deliver us from evil,
For thine is the kingdom, and the power, and the glory, for ever.
Amen.

GOD IS NOT DUMB

James Russell Lowell

God is not dumb, that He should speak no more;
  If thou hast wanderings in the wilderness
And findest not Sinai, 'tis thy soul is poor;
  There towers the Mountain of the Voice no less,
Which whoso seeks shall find; but he who bends,
Intent on manna still and mortal ends,
  Sees it not, neither hears its thundered lore.

Slowly the Bible of the race is writ,
  And not on paper leaves nor leaves of stone;
Each age, each kindred, adds a verse to it,
  Texts of despair and hope, of joy or moan.
While swings the sea, while mists the mountains
    shroud
  While thunders' surges burst on cliff of cloud,
Still at the prophets' feet the nations sit.

PIED BEAUTY

Gerard Manley Hopkins

GLORY BE to God for dappled things—
For skies of couple-colour as a brinded cow;
For rose-moles all in stipple upon trout that swim;
Fresh-firecoal chestnut-falls; finches' wings;
Landscape plotted and pieced—fold, fallow, and plough;
And all trades, their gear and tackle and trim.

All things counter, original, spare, strange;
Whatever is fickle, freckled (who knows how?)
With swift, slow; sweet, sour; adazzle, dim;
He fathers-forth whose beauty is past change:
Praise him.

THE PILLAR OF THE CLOUD

John Henry Newman

LEAD, KINDLY light, amid the encircling gloom,
Lead thou me on!
The night is dark and I am far from home;
Lead thou me on!
Keep thou my feet; I do not ask to see
The distant scene; one step enough for me.

I was not ever thus, nor prayed that thou
Shouldst lead me on;
I loved to choose and see my path; but now
Lead thou me on!
I loved the garish day, and, spite of fears
Pride ruled my will: remember not past years!

So long thy power has blest me, sure it still
Will lead me on
O'er moor and fen, o'er crag and torrent till
The night is gone,
And with the morn those angel faces smile
Which I have loved long since and lost awhile!

ROCKED IN THE CRADLE OF THE DEEP

Emma Willard

ROCKED in the cradle of the deep
I lay me down in peace to sleep;
Secure I rest upon the wave,
For thou, O Lord, hast power to save.
I know thou wilt not slight my call,
For thou dost mark the sparrow's fall;
And calm and peaceful shall I sleep,
Rocked in the cradle of the deep.

When in the dead of night I lie
And gaze upon the trackless sky,
The star-bespangled heavenly scroll,
The boundless waters as they roll,—
I feel thy wondrous power to save
From perils of the stormy wave:
Rocked in the cradle of the deep
I calmly rest and soundly sleep.

And such the trust that still were mine,
Though stormy winds swept o'er the brine,
Or though the tempest's fiery breath
Roused me from sleep to wreck and death.
In ocean cave still safe with Thee
The gem of immortality!
And calm and peaceful shall I sleep
Rocked in the cradle of the deep.

ONWARD, CHRISTIAN SOLDIERS

Sabine Baring-Gould

ONWARD, Christian soldiers,
Marching as to war,
With the cross of Jesus
Going on before.
Christ the royal master,
Leads against the foe;
Forward into battle,
See his banners go.

At the sound of triumph
Satan's host doth flee;
On, then, Christian soldiers,
On to victory!
Hell's foundations quiver
At the shout of praise;
Brothers lift your voices,
Loud your anthems raise.

Like a mighty army
Moves the church of God;
Brethren, we are treading
Where the saints have trod;
We are not divided,
All one body, we,
One in hope and doctrine,
One in charity.

Crowns and thrones may perish,
  Kingdoms rise and wane,
But the church of Jesus
  Constant will remain;
Gates of hell can never
  'Gainst that church prevail;
We have Christ's own promise,
  And that cannot fail.

Onward, therefore, pilgrim brothers,
  Onward with the cross our aid!
Bear its shame and fight its battle,
  Till we rest beneath its shade!
Soon shall come the great awaking,
  Soon the rending of the tomb;
Then the scattering of the shadows,
  And the end of toil and gloom.

THE HOUSE BY THE SIDE OF THE ROAD

Sam Walter Foss

THERE ARE hermit souls that live withdrawn
In the peace of their self-content;
There are souls, like stars, that dwell apart
In a fellowless firmament;
There are pioneer souls that blaze their paths
Where highways never ran–
But let me live by the side of the road
And be a friend to man.

Let me live in a house by the side of the road,
Where the race of men go by–
The men who are good and the men who are bad,
As good and as bad as I.
I would not sit in the scorner's seat,
Or hurl the cynic's ban–
Let me live in a house by the side of the road,
And be a friend to man.

I see from my house by the side of the road,
By the side of the highway of life,
The men who press with the ardor of hope
The men who are faint with the strife.
But I turn not away from their smiles nor their tears–
Both parts of an infinite plan–
Let me live in a house by the side of the road
And be a friend to man.

I know there are brook-gladdened meadows ahead
 And mountains of wearisome height;
And the road passes on through the long afternoon
 And stretches away to the night.
But still I rejoice when the travelers rejoice,
 And weep with the strangers that moan,
Nor live in my house by the side of the road
 Like a man who dwells alone.

Let me live in my house by the side of the road
 Where the race of men go by–
They are good, they are bad, they are weak, they are
 strong,
 Wise, foolish–so am I.
Then why should I sit in the scorner's seat
 Or hurl the cynic's ban?
Let me live in my house by the side of the road
 And be a friend to man.

BATTLE HYMN OF THE REPUBLIC

Julia Ward Howe

MINE EYES have seen the glory of the coming of the Lord:
He is trampling out the vintage where the grapes of wrath are stored;
He hath loosed the fateful lightning of His terrible swift sword:
His truth is marching on.

I have seen Him in the watch-fires of a hundred circling camps,
They have builded Him an altar in the evening dews and damps;
I can read His righteous sentence by the dim and flaring lamps:
His day is marching on.

I have read a fiery gospel writ in burnished rows of steel:
"As ye deal with my contemners so with you my grace shall deal;
Let the Hero, born of woman, crush the serpent with his heel,
Since God is marching on!"

He has sounded forth the trumpet that shall never call retreat;
He is sifting out the hearts of men before His judgment seat.

Oh, be swift, my soul, to answer Him! be jubilant,
 my feet:
 Our God is marching on.

In the beauty of the lilies Christ was born across the
 sea,
With a glory in His bosom that transfigures you and
 me;
As He died to make men holy, let us die to make men
 free,
 While God is marching on.

ROCK OF AGES

Augustus M. Toplady

Rock of Ages, cleft for me,
Let me hide myself in thee;
Let the water and the blood,
From thy wounded side which flowed,
Be of sin the double cure,
Save from wrath and make me pure.

Could my tears forever flow,
Could my zeal no languor know,
These for sin could not atone;
Thou must save and thou alone:
In my hand no price I bring;
Simply to thy cross I cling.

While I draw this fleeting breath,
When my eyes shall close in death,
When I rise to worlds unknown,
And behold thee on thy throne,
Rock of Ages, cleft for me,
Let me hide myself in thee.

THE MAN WITH THE HOE

Edwin Markham

BOWED BY the weight of centuries, he leans
Upon his hoe and gazes on the ground,
The emptiness of ages in his face,
And on his back the burden of the world.
Who made him dead to rapture and despair,
A thing that grieves not and that never hopes,
Stolid and stunned, a brother to the ox?
Who loosened and let down this brutal jaw?
Whose was the hand that slanted back this brow?
Whose breath blew out the light within this brain?

Is this the Thing the Lord God made and gave
To have dominion over sea and land;
To trace the stars and search the heavens for power;
To feel the passion of Eternity?
Is this the Dream He dreamed who shaped the suns
And pillared the blue firmament with light?
Down all the stretch of Hell to its last gulf,
There is no shape more terrible than this–
More tongued with censure of the world's blind greed–
More filled with signs and portents for the soul–
More fraught with menace to the universe.

What gulfs between him and the seraphim!
Slave of the wheel of labour, what to him

Are Plato and the swing of Pleiades?
What the long reaches of the peaks of song,
The rift of dawn, the reddening of the rose?
Through this dread shape the suffering ages look;
Time's tragedy is in that aching stoop;
Through this dread shape humanity betrayed,
Plundered, profaned, and disinherited,
Cries protest to the Judges of the World,
A protest that is also prophesy.

O masters, lords and rulers in all lands,
Is this the handiwork you give to God,
This monstrous thing distorted and soul-quenched?
How will you ever straighten up this shape;
Touch it again with immortality;
Give back the upward looking and the light;
Rebuild in it the music and the dream;
Make right the immemorial infamies,
Perfidious wrongs, immedicable woes?

O masters, lords, and rulers in all lands,
How will the Future reckon with this Man?
How answer his brute questions in that hour
When whirlwinds of rebellion shake the world?
How will it be with kingdoms and with kings—
With those who shaped him to the thing he is—
When this dumb Terror shall reply to God
After the silence of the centuries?

VESPERS

Silas Weir Mitchell

I KNOW the night is near at hand:
The mists lie low on hill and bay,
The Autumn sheaves are dewless, dry;
But I have had the day.

Yes, I have had, dear Lord, the day;
When at thy call I have the night,
Brief be the twilight as I pass
From light to dark, from dark to light.

FOR INSPIRATION

Michelangelo Buonarotti

Translated by WILLIAM WORDSWORTH

THE PRAYERS I make will then be sweet indeed,
If thou the spirit give by which I pray;
My unassisted heart is barren clay,
Which of its native self can nothing feed;
Of good and pious works thou art the seed
Which quickens where thou say'st it may;
Unless thou show us then thine own true way,
No man can find it! Father, Thou must lead!
Do thou, then, breathe those thoughts into my mind
By which such virtue may in me be bred
That in thy holy footsteps I may tread:
The fetters of my tongue do thou unbind,
That I may have the power to sing of thee
And sound thy praises everlastingly.

THE WAY, THE TRUTH, AND THE LIFE

Theodore Parker

O THOU great Friend to all the sons of men,
Who once appear'dst in humblest guise below,
Sin to rebuke, to break the captive's chain,
To call thy brethren forth from want and woe!–
Thee would I sing. Thy truth is still the light
Which guides the nations groping on their way,
Stumbling and falling in disastrous night,
Yet hoping ever for the perfect day.

Yes, thou art still the life; thou art the way
The holiest know,–light, life, and way of heaven;
And they who dearest hope and deepest pray
Toil by the truth, life, way that thou hast given;
And in thy name aspiring mortals trust
To uplift their bleeding brothers rescued from the dust.

THE CHERUBIC PILGRIM

Johannes Scheffler

THE SOUL wherein God dwells,–
  What church could holier be?–
Becomes a walking tent
  Of heavenly majesty.

How far from here to Heaven?
  Not very far, my friend,
A single hearty step
  Will all thy journey end.

Though Christ a thousand times
  In Bethlehem be born,
If He's not born in thee,
  Thy soul is still forlorn.

The cross on Golgotha
  Will never save thy soul,
The cross in thine own heart
  Alone can make thee whole.

Hold there! where runnest thou?
  Know Heaven is in thee.
Seek'st thou for God elsewhere,
  His face thou'lt never see.

O, would thy heart but be
  A manger for His birth;

God would once more become
   A child upon the earth.

Go out, God will go in,
   Die thou and let Him live.
Be not–and He will be.
   Wait and He'll all things give.

O shame, a silk worm works
   And spins till it can fly,
And thou, my soul, wilt still
   On thine old earth-clod lie!

HYMN

St. Thomas Aquinas

SING, MY tongue, the Saviour's glory,
Of His flesh the mystery sing;
Of the blood, all price exceeding,
Shed by our Immortal King.
Destined for the world's redemption,
From the noble womb to spring.

Of a pure and spotless Virgin
Born for us on earth below,
He, as Man with man conversing,
Stayed the seeds of truth to sow;
Then He closed in solemn order
Wondrously His life of woe.

On the night of that Last Supper,
Seated with His chosen band,
He the paschal victim eating,
First fulfils the Law's command;
Then, as food to all His brethren,
Gives Himself with His own Hand.

Word made flesh, the bread of nature
By His Word to Flesh He turns;
Wine into His Blood He changes:–
What though sense no change discerns,
Only be the heart in earnest,
Faith her lesson quickly learns.

Down in adoration falling,
Lo! the Sacred Host we hail:
Lo! o'er ancient forms departing,
Newer rites of grace prevail:
Faith for all defects supplying,
Where the feeble senses fail.

To the Everlasting Father,
And the Son who reigns on high,
With the Holy Ghost proceeding
Forth from each eternally,
Be salvation, honour, blessing,
Might and endless majesty. Amen.

THE INNER CALM

Horatius Bonar

CALM ME, my God, and keep me calm,
  While these hot breezes blow;
Be like the night-dew's cooling balm
  Upon earth's fevered brow.

Calm me, my God, and keep me calm,
  Soft resting on thy breast;
Soothe me with holy hymn and psalm
  And bid my spirit rest.

Yes, keep me calm, though loud and rude
  The sounds my ear that greet;
Calm in the closet's solitude,
  Calm in the bustling street;

Calm in the hour of buoyant health,
  Calm in my hour of pain,
Calm in my poverty or wealth,
  Calm in my loss or gain;

Calm when the great world's news with power
  My listening spirit stir;
Let not the tidings of the hour
  E'er find too fond an ear;

Calm as the ray of sun or star
  Which storms assail in vain;
Moving unruffled through earth's war,
  The eternal calm to gain.

TREES

Joyce Kilmer

I THINK that I shall never see
A poem lovely as a tree.

A tree whose hungry mouth is pressed
Against the earth's sweet flowing breast;

A tree that looks at God all day,
And lifts her leafy arms to pray;

A tree that may in summer wear
A nest of robins in her hair;

Upon whose bosom snow has lain;
Who intimately lives with rain.

Poems are made by fools like me,
But only God can make a tree.

From *Trees and Other Poems* by Joyce Kilmer. Reprinted by permission of Doubleday and Company, Inc., publishers.

SONG OF MYSELF

Walt Whitman

I HEAR and behold God in every object, yet understand God not in the least,
Nor do I understand who there can be more wonderful than myself.

Why should I wish to see God better than this day?
I see something of God each hour of the twenty-four, and each moment then,

In the faces of men and women I see God, and in my own face in the glass,
I find letters from God dropped in the street–and every one is signed by God's name,
And I leave them where they are, for I know that others will punctually come forever and ever.

THE ELIXIR

George Herbert

TEACH ME, my God and King,
  In all things thee to see,
And what I do in anything
  To do it as for thee.

Not rudely, as a beast,
  To run into an action;
But still to make thee prepossest,
  And give it his perfection.

A man that looks on glass,
  On it may stay his eye;
Or, if he pleaseth, through it pass,
  And then the heaven espy.

All may of thee partake:
  Nothing can be so mean
Which with his tincture (for thy sake)
  Will not grow bright and clean.

A servant makes this clause
  Makes drudgery divine;
Who sweeps a room as for thy laws
  Makes that and the action fine.

This is the famous stone
  That turneth all to gold;
For that which God doth touch and own
  Cannot for less be told.

O GOD, OUR HELP IN AGES PAST

Isaac Watts

O God, our help in ages past,
 Our hope in years to come,
Our shelter from the stormy blast,
 And our eternal home–

Under the shadow of thy throne
 Thy saints have dwelt secure;
Sufficient is thine arm alone,
 And our defense is sure.

Before the hills in order stood,
 Or earth received her frame,
From everlasting thou art God,
 To endless years the same.

A thousand ages in thy sight
 Are like an evening gone;
Short as the watch that ends the night
 Before the rising sun.

Time, like an ever-rolling stream
 Bears all its sons away;
They fly, forgotten, as a dream
 Dies at the opening day.

Our God, our help in ages past,
 Our hope in years to come,
Be thou our guard while troubles last,
 And our eternal home.

THE CITY OF GOD

Francis Turner Palgrave

O Thou not made with hands,
Not throned above the skies,
Nor wall'd with shining walls,
Nor framed with stones of price,
  More bright than gold or gem,
  God's own Jerusalem!

Where'er the gentle heart
Finds courage from above;
Where'er the heart forsook
Warms with the breath of love;
  Where faith bids fear depart,
  City of God! thou art.

Thou art where'er the proud
In humbleness melts down;
Where self itself yields up;
Where martyrs win their crown;
  Where faithful souls possess
  Themselves in perfect peace.

Where in life's common ways
With cheerful feet we go;
When in His steps we tread
Who trod the way of woe;
  Where He is in the heart,
  City of God! thou art.

Not throned above the skies,
Nor golden-wall'd afar,
But where Christ's two or three
In His name gather'd are,
  Be in the midst of them,
  God's own Jerusalem!

BETTER THAN GOLD

Abram J. Ryan

BETTER THAN grandeur, better than gold,
Than rank and titles a thousandfold,
Is a healthy body, a mind at ease,
And simple pleasures that always please;
A heart that can feel for another's woe,
That has learned with love's deep fires to glow,
With sympathy large enough to enfold
All men as brothers, is better than gold.

Better than gold is a conscience clear,
Though toiling for bread in a humble sphere;
Doubly blest is content and health
Untried by the lusts and the cares of wealth.
Lowly living and lofty thought
Adorn and ennoble the poor man's cot;
For mind and morals in nature's plan
Are the genuine tests of the gentleman.

Better than gold is the sweet repose
Of the sons of toil when labors close;
Better than gold is the poor man's sleep
And the balm that drops on his slumbers deep.
Bring sleeping draughts to the downy bed,
Where luxury pillows its aching head;
The toiler a simple opiate deems
A shorter route to the land of dreams.

Better than gold is a thinking mind
That in the realm of books can find
A treasure surpassing Australian ore,
And live with the great and good of yore;
The sage's lore and the poet's lay;
The glories of empires passed away;
The world's great dream will thus unfold
And yield a pleasure better than gold.

Better than gold is a peaceful home,
Where all the fireside characters come,
The shrine of love, the heaven of life,
Hallowed by mother or by wife.
However humble the home may be,
Or tried with sorrow by heaven's decree,
The blessings that never were bought or sold
And center there, are better than gold.

LAST LINES

Emily Brontë

No COWARD soul is mine,
No trembler in the world's storm-troubled sphere;
I see Heaven's glories shine,
And faith shines equal, arming me from fear.

O God within my breast,
Almighty, ever-present Deity!
Life–that in me has rest,
As I–undying life–have power in thee!

Vain are the thousand creeds
That move men's hearts: unutterably vain;
Worthless as withered weeds,
Or idlest froth amid the boundless main.

To waken doubt in one
Holding so fast by thine infinity;
So surely anchored on
The steadfast rock of immortality.

With wide-embracing love
Thy Spirit animates eternal years,
Pervades and broods above,
Changes, sustains, dissolves, creates and rears.

Though earth and man were gone,
And suns and universes ceased to be,
And Thou were left alone,
Every existence would exist in Thee.

There is not room for Death
Nor atom that his might could render void:
Thou–Thou art Being and Breath,
And what Thou art may never be destroyed.

CROSSING THE BAR

Alfred Tennyson

SUNSET AND evening star,
And one clear call for me!
And may there be no moaning of the bar,
When I put out to sea.

But such a tide as moving seems asleep,
Too full for sound and foam,
When that which drew from out the boundless deep
Turns again home.

Twilight and evening bell,
And after that, the dark!
And may there be no sadness of farewell,
When I embark;

For tho' from out our bourne of Time and Place
The flood may bear me far,
I hope to see my Pilot face to face
When I have crossed the bar.

SPEAK OUT

IF YOU have a friend worth loving,
Love him. Yes, and let him know
That you love him, ere life's evening
Tinge his brow with sunset glow.
Why should good words ne'er be said
Of a friend–till he is dead?

If you hear a song that thrills you,
Sung by any child of song,
Praise it. Do not let the singer
Wait deserved praises long.
Why should one who thrills your heart
Lack the joy you may impart?

If you hear a prayer that moves you
By its humble, pleading tone,
Join it. Do not let the seeker
Bow before his God alone.
Why should not thy brother share
The strength of "two or three" in prayer?

If your work is made more easy
By a friendly, helping hand,
Say so. Speak out brave and truly,
Ere the darkness veil the land.
Should a brother workman dear
Falter for a word of cheer?

Scatter thus your seeds of kindness
All enriching as you go–
Leave them. Trust the Harvest-Giver;
He will make each seed to grow.
So, until the happy end,
Your life shall never lack a friend.

THE CONCLUSION

Sir Walter Raleigh

EVEN SUCH is time, that takes in trust
Our youth, our joys, are all we have,
And pays us but with earth and dust;
Who, in the dark and silent grave,
When we have wandered all our ways,
Shuts up the story of our days;
But from this earth, this grave, this dust,
My God shall raise me up, I trust.

ABOU BEN ADHEM

Leigh Hunt

Abou Ben Adhem (may his tribe increase!)
Awoke one night from a deep dream of peace,
And saw within the moonlight in his room,
Making it rich and like a lily in bloom,
An angel writing in a book of gold;
Exceeding peace had made Ben Adhem bold,
And to the Presence in the room he said,
"What writest thou?" The vision raised its head,
And with a look made of all sweet accord,
Answered, "The names of those who love the Lord."
"And is mine one?" said Abou. "Nay, not so,"
Replied the angel. Abou spoke more low,
But cheerly still, and said, "I pray thee, then,
Write me as one who loves his fellow-men."
The angel wrote and vanished; the next night
It came again with a great wakening light,
And showed their names whom love of God hath blest,
And lo! Ben Adhem's name led all the rest.

COME, YE DISCONSOLATE

Thomas Moore

COME, YE disconsolate, where'er you languish,
Come, at God's altar fervently kneel;
Here bring your wounded hearts, here tell your anguish,–
Earth has no sorrow that heaven cannot heal.

Joy of the desolate, light of the straying,
Hope when all others die, fadeless and pure,
Here speaks the comforter, in God's name saying,
"Earth has no sorrow that heaven cannot cure."

Go, ask the infidel what boon he brings us,
What charm for aching hearts he can reveal,
Sweet as that heavenly promise hope sings us,–
"Earth has no sorrow that God cannot heal."

WHEN I HAVE TIME

WHEN I have time so many things I'll do
To make life happier and more fair
For those whose lives are crowded now with care;
I'll help to lift them from their low despair
  When I have time.

When I have time the friend I love so well
Shall know no more these weary, toiling days;
I'll lead her feet in pleasant paths always
And cheer her heart with words of sweetest praise,
  When I have time.

When you have time! The friend you hold so dear
May be beyond the reach of all your sweet intent;
May never know that you so kindly meant
To fill her life with sweet content
  When you had time.

Now is the time! Ah, friend, no longer wait
To scatter loving smiles and words of cheer
To those around whose lives are now so drear;
They may not need you in the coming year–
  Now is the time!

THE CHRISTIAN LIFE

Samuel Longfellow

I LOOK to Thee in ev'ry need,
  And never look in vain;
I feel Thy strong and tender love,
  And all is well again;
The thought of Thee is mightier far
Than sin and pain and sorrow are.

Discouraged in the work of life,
  Disheartened by its load,
Shamed by its failures or its fears,
  I sink beside the road;
But let me only think of Thee,
And then new heart springs up in me.

Thy calmness bends serene above,
  My restlessness to still,
Around me flows Thy quickening life
  To nerve my faltering will;
Thy presence fills my solitude,
Thy providence turns all to good.

Embosomed deep in Thy great love,
  Held in Thy law, I stand;
Thy hand in all things I behold,
  And all things in Thy hand;
Thou leadest me by unsought ways,
And turn'st my mourning into praise.

SONNET ON HIS BLINDNESS

John Milton

WHEN I consider how my light is spent
Ere half my days in this dark world and wide,
And that one talent which is death to hide,
Lodged with me useless, though my soul more bent
To serve therewith my Maker, and present
My true account, lest he returning chide;
"Doth God exact day-labor, light denied?"
I fondly ask. But Patience, to prevent
That murmur, soon replies, "God doth not need
Either man's work or his own gifts; who best
Bear his mild yoke, they serve him best; his state
Is kingly: thousands at his bidding speed,
And post o'er land and ocean without rest;
They also serve who only stand and wait."

THE ANGEL OF PATIENCE

John Greenleaf Whittier

To WEARY hearts, to mourning homes
God's meekest angel gently comes:
No power has he to banish pain,
Or give us back our lost again;
And yet in tenderest love, our dear
And Heavenly Father sends him here.

There's quiet in the angel's glance,
There's rest in his still countenance!
He mocks no grief with idle cheer,
Nor wounds with words the mourner's ear;
But ills and woes he may not cure
He kindly trains us to endure.

SOCIAL CHRISTIANITY

O FOR a closer walk with man!
  Sweet fellowship of soul,
Where each is to the other bound,
  Parts of one living whole.

Our Father, God, help us to see
  That all in thee are one;
O warm our hearts with thy pure love,
  Strong as your glorious sun.

Pride, envy, selfishness will melt
  Beneath that kindling fire;
Our brother's faults we scarce shall see,
  But good in all admire.

No bitter cry of misery
  Shall ever pass unheard;
But gentle sympathy spring forth
  In smile and strengthening word.

And when our brother's voice shall call
  From lands beyond the sea,
Our hearts in glad response will say,
  "Here, Lord, am I, send me."

O Jesus Christ, thou who wast man,
  Grant us thy face to see;
In thy light shall we understand
  What human life may be.

Then daily with thy Spirit filled,
According to thy word,
New power shall flow through us to all,
And draw men near our Lord.

Thus will the deep desire be met
With which our prayer began;
A closer walk with Thee will mean
A closer walk with man.

THE CELESTIAL SURGEON

Robert Louis Stevenson

IF I HAVE faltered more or less
In my great task of happiness;
If I have moved among my race
And shown no glorious morning face;
If beams from happy human eyes
Have moved me not; if morning skies,
Books and my food, and summer rain
Knocked on my sullen heart in vain:–
Lord, Thy most pointed pleasure take
And stab my spirit broad awake!
Or, Lord, if too obdurate I,
Choose Thou, before that spirit die,
A piercing pain, a killing sin
And to my dead heart run them in!

'TIS SORROW BUILDS THE SHINING LADDER UP

James Russell Lowell

'Tis sorrow builds the shining ladder up,
Whose golden rounds are our calamities,
Whereon our feet planting, nearer God
The spirit climbs and hath its eyes unsealed.

True it is that Death's face seems stern and cold,
When he is sent to summon those we love,
But all God's angels come to us disguised.
Sorrow and sickness, poverty and death,
One after other lift their frowning masks
And we behold the seraph's face beneath,
All radiant with the glory and the calm
Of having looked upon the front of God.
With every anguish of our earthly part
The spirit's path grows clearer; this was meant
When Jesus touched the blind man's lids with clay.
Life is the jailer; Death the angel sent
To draw the unwilling bolts and set us free.

THE LOST CHORD

Adelaide Anne Proctor

SEATED ONE day at the Organ,
  I was weary and ill at ease,
And my fingers wandered idly
  Over the noisy keys.

I know not what I was playing,
  Or what I was dreaming then;
But I struck one chord of music,
  Like the sound of a great Amen.

It flooded the crimson twilight,
  Like the close of an angel's Psalm,
And it lay on my fevered spirit
  With a touch of infinite calm.

It quieted pain and sorrow,
  Like love overcoming strife;
It seemed the harmonious echo
  From our discordant life.

It linked all perplexed meanings
  Into one perfect peace,
And trembled away into silence
  As if it were loth to cease.

I have sought but I seek it vainly,
  That one lost chord divine,
Which came from the soul of the Organ
  And entered into mine.

It may be that Death's bright angel
Will speak in that chord again–
It may be that only in Heaven
I shall hear that great Amen.

A CALL TO NATURE AND ALL MEN TO PRAISE GOD

Psalm 148

PRAISE YE the Lord.
Praise ye the Lord from the heavens: praise him in the heights.
Praise ye him, all his angels: praise ye him, all his hosts.
Praise ye him, sun and moon: praise him, all ye stars of light.
Praise him, ye heavens of heavens, and ye waters that be above the heavens.
Let them praise the name of the Lord,
For he commanded, and they were created.
He hath also stablished them for ever and ever.
He hath made a decree which shall not pass.
Praise the Lord from the earth, ye dragons, and all deeps:
Fire, and hail; snow, and vapours; stormy wind fulfilling his word:
Mountains, and all hills; fruitful trees, and all cedars:
Beasts, and all cattle; creeping things, and flying fowl:
Kings of the earth, and all people; princes, and all judges of the earth:
Both young men, and maidens; old men, and children:
Let them praise the name of the Lord.
For his name alone is excellent; his glory is above the earth and heaven.

He also exalteth the horn of his people, the praise of
all his saints;
Even of the children of Israel, a people near unto him.
Praise ye the Lord.

THE CRUCIFIXION

Negro Spiritual

THEY crucified my Lord,
  And He never said a mumbaling word.
They crucified my Lord,
  And He never said a mumbaling word.
Not a word–not a word–not a word.

They nailed Him to the tree,
  And He never said a mumbaling word.
They nailed Him to the tree,
  And He never said a mumbaling word.
Not a word–not a word–not a word.

They pierced Him in the side,
  And He never said a mumbaling word.
They pierced Him in the side,
  And He never said a mumbaling word.
Not a word–not a word–not a word.

The blood came twinkaling down,
  And He never said a mumbaling word.
The blood came twinkaling down,
  And He never said a mumbaling word.
Not a word–not a word–not a word.

He bowed His head and died,
  And He never said a mumbaling word.
He bowed His head and died,
  And He never said a mumbaling word!
Not a word–not a word–not a word.

STEAL AWAY

Negro Spiritual

STEAL AWAY, steal away, steal away to Jesus.
Steal away, steal away home,
I ain't got long to stay here.

My Lord, He calls me,
He calls me by the thunder,
The trumpet sounds within-a my soul;
I ain't got long to stay here.

Steal away, steal away, steal away to Jesus,
Steal away, steal away home,
I ain't got long to stay here.

Green trees a-bending,
Po' sinner stands a-trembling
The trumpet sounds within-a my soul;
I ain't got long to stay here.

Steal away, steal away, steal away to Jesus.
Steal away, steal away home,
I ain't got long to stay here.

HORA CHRISTI

Alice Brown

SWEET IS the time for joyous folk
Of gifts and minstrelsy;
Yet, I, O lowly-hearted One
Crave but Thy company,
O lonesome road, beset with dread,
My questing lies afar,
I have no light save in the east,
The gleaming of Thy Star.

In cloistered aisles they keep today
Thy feast, O living Lord!
With pomp of banner, pride of song,
And stately sounding word.
Mute stand the kings of power and place,
While priests of holy mind
Dispense Thy blessed heritage
Of peace to all mankind.

I know a spot where budless twigs
Are bare above the snow,
And where sweet winter-loving birds
Flit softly to and fro;
There, with the sun for altar-fire,
The earth for kneeling-place,
The gentle air for chorister,
Will I adore Thy face.

Lord, underneath the great blue sky,
My heart shall pean sing,
The gold and myrrh of meekest love
Mine only offering.
Bliss of Thy birth shall quicken me,
And for Thy pain and dole
Tears are but vain, so I will keep
The silence of the soul.

NOT IN DUMB RESIGNATION

John Hay

Not in dumb resignation,
  We lift our hands on high;
Not like the nerveless fatalist,
  Content to trust and die.
Our faith springs like the eagle,
  Who soars to meet the sun,
And cries exulting unto Thee,
  "O Lord, thy will be done!"

When tyrant feet are trampling
  Upon the common weal,
Thou dost not bid us bend and writhe
  Beneath the iron heel;
In Thy name we assert our right
  By sword or tongue or pen,
And even the headsman's axe may flash
  Thy message unto men.

Thy will,–it strengthens weakness;
  It bids the strong be just:
No lip to fawn, no hand to beg,
  No brow to seek the dust.
Wherever man oppresses man
  Beneath the liberal sun,
O Lord, be there, Thine arm made bare,
  Thy righteous will be done.

O MASTER, LET ME WALK WITH THEE

Washington Gladden

O Master, let me walk with Thee
In lowly paths of service free;
Tell me Thy secret; help me bear
The strain of toil, the fret of care.

Help me the slow of heart to move
By some clear winning word of love,
Teach me the wayward feet to stay,
And guide them in the homeward way.

Teach me Thy patience; still with Thee
In closer, dearer company,
In work that keeps faith sweet and strong,
In trust that triumphs over wrong.

In hope that sends a shining ray
Far down the future's broadening way;
In peace that only Thou canst give,
With Thee, O Master, let me live.

CHILD'S EVENING HYMN

Sabine Baring-Gould

NOW THE day is over,
  Night is drawing nigh,
Shadows of the evening
  Steal across the sky.

Now the darkness gathers,
  Stars begin to peep,
Birds and beasts and flowers
  Soon will be asleep.

Jesus give the weary
  Calm and sweet repose,
With thy tenderest blessing
  May our eyelids close.

Grant to little children
  Visions bright of thee,
Guard the sailors tossing
  On the deep blue sea.

Comfort every sufferer
  Watching late in pain;
Those who plan some evil
  From their sin restrain.

Through the long night-watches
  May thy angels spread

Their white wings above me,
Watching round my bed.

When the morning wakens,
Then may I arise
Pure and fresh and sinless
In thy holy eyes.

REVELATION

Edwin Markham

I MADE A pilgrimage to find the God:
I listened for His voice at holy tombs,
Searched for the print of His immortal feet
In dust of broken altars: yet turned back
With empty heart. But on the homeward road,
A great light came upon me, and I heard
The God's voice singing in a nestling lark;
Felt his sweet wonder in a swaying rose;
Received his blessing from a wayside well;
Looked on his beauty in a lover's face;
Saw his bright hand send signals from the suns.

A TRAVELER'S HYMN OF TRUST IN JEHOVAH

Psalm 121

I WILL LIFT up mine eyes unto the hills, from whence cometh my help.

My help cometh from the Lord, which made heaven and earth.

He will not suffer thy foot to be moved: he that keepeth thee will not slumber.

Behold, he that keepeth Israel shall neither slumber nor sleep.

The Lord is thy keeper: the Lord is thy shade upon thy right hand.

The sun shall not smite thee by day, nor the moon by night.

The Lord shall preserve thee from all evil: he shall preserve thy soul.

The Lord shall preserve thy going out and thy coming in from this time forth, and even for evermore.

A SUN-DAY HYMN

Oliver Wendell Holmes

LORD OF all being, throned afar,
Thy glory flames from sun and star:
Center and soul of every sphere,
Yet to each loving heart how near!

Sun of our life, thy quickening ray
Sheds on our path the glow of day;
Star of our hope, thy softened light
Cheers the long watches of the night.

Our midnight is thy smile withdrawn;
Our noontide is thy gracious dawn;
Our rainbow arch thy mercy's sign;
All, save the clouds of sin, are thine.

Lord of all life, below, above
Whose light is truth, whose warmth is love,
Before thy ever-blazing throne
We ask no luster of our own.

Grant us thy truth to make us free,
And kindling hearts that burn for thee,
Till all thy living altars claim
One holy light, one heavenly flame.

ABIDE WITH ME

Henry F. Lyte

ABIDE WITH me! Fast falls the eventide,
The darkness deepens: Lord, with me abide!
When other helpers fail, and comforts flee,
Help of the helpless, O, abide with me!

Swift to its close ebbs out life's little day;
Earth's joys grow dim, its glories pass away;
Change and decay in all around I see;
O thou, who changest not, abide with me!

I need thy presence every passing hour;
What but thy grace can foil the tempter's power?
Who, like thyself, my guide and stay can be?
Through cloud and sunshine, Lord, abide with me!

I fear no foe, with thee at hand to bless;
Ills have no weight, and tears no bitterness;
Where is death's sting? where, grave, thy victory?
I triumph still, if thou abide with me.

Hold thou thy cross before my closing eyes;
Shine through the gloom and point me to the skies;
Heaven's morning breaks, and earth's vain shadows flee
In life, in death, O Lord, abide with me!

LIFT UP YOUR HEADS, REJOICE!

Thomas T. Lynch

LIFT UP your heads, rejoice,
  Redemption draweth nigh!
Now breathes a softer air,
  Now shines a milder sky;
The early trees put forth
  Their new and tender leaf;
Hushed is the moaning wind
  That told of winter's grief.

Lift up your heads, rejoice,
  Redemption draweth nigh!
Now mount the leaden clouds,
  Now flames the darkening sky;
The early scattered drops
  Descend with heavy fall,
And to the waiting earth
  The hidden thunders call.

Lift up your heads, rejoice,
  Redemption draweth nigh!
O note the varying signs
  Of earth, and air, and sky;
The God of glory comes
  In gentleness and might,
To comfort and alarm,
  To succor and to smite.

He comes, the wide world's King,
He comes, the true heart's Friend,
New gladness to begin,
And ancient wrong to end;
He comes, to fill with light
The weary waiting eye:
Lift up your heads, rejoice,
Redemption draweth nigh.

UNCONQUERED

(INVICTUS)

William Ernest Henley

OUT OF the night that covers me,
Black as the pit from pole to pole,
I thank whatever gods may be
For my unconquerable soul.

Beyond this place of wrath and tears
Looms but the horror of the shade,
And yet the menace of the years
Finds and shall find me unafraid.

In the fell clutch of circumstance
I have not winced nor cried aloud;
Under the bludgeonings of chance
My head is bloody, but unbowed.

It matters not how strait the gate,
How charged with punishments the scroll;
I am the master of my fate,
I am the captain of my soul.

FROM GREENLAND'S ICY MOUNTAINS

Reginald Heber

FROM Greenland's icy mountains,
  From India's coral strand,
Where Afric's sunny fountains
  Roll down their golden sand,
From many an ancient river,
  From many a palmy plain,
They call us to deliver
  Their land from error's chain.

What though the spicy breezes
  Blow soft o'er Ceylon's isle;
Though every prospect pleases,
  And only man is vile;
In vain, with lavish kindness,
  The gifts of God are strown;
The heathen in his blindness,
  Bows down to wood and stone.

Can we, whose souls are lighted
  With wisdom from on high,–
Can we to men benighted
  The lamp of life deny?
Salvation! O salvation!
  The joyful sound proclaim,
Till each remotest nation
  Has learned Messiah's name.

Waft, waft, ye winds, His story;
  And you, ye waters, roll,
Till like a sea of glory,
  It spreads from pole to pole;
Till, o'er our ransomed nature,
  The Lamb for sinners slain
Redeemer, King, Creator,
  In bliss return to reign.

ADESTE FIDELES

Translated by FREDERICK OAKELEY

O COME, all ye faithful,
Joyful and triumphant;
O come ye, O come ye to Bethlehem;
Come and behold Him
Born, the King of Angels;
O come, let us adore Him,
O come, let us adore Him,
O come, let us adore Him, Christ the Lord.

God of God,
Light of Light,
Lo! He abhors not the Virgin's womb;
Very God,
Begotten, not created;
O come, let us adore Him,
O come, let us adore Him,
O come, let us adore Him, Christ the Lord.

Sing, choirs of angels;
Sing in exultation,
Sing, all ye citizens of Heav'n above:
"Glory to God
All glory in the highest";
O come, let us adore Him,
O come, let us adore Him,
O come, let us adore Him, Christ the Lord.

Yea, Lord, we greet Thee,
Born this happy morning;
Jesu, to Thee be glory given:
Word of the Father,
Now in flesh appearing;
O come, let us adore Him,
O come, let us adore Him,
O come, let us adore Him, Christ the Lord.

ISRAEL LOOKS FOR VINDICATION FROM JEHOVAH

Psalm 98

O SING unto the Lord a new song; for he hath done marvellous things: his right hand, and his holy arm, hath gotten him the victory.

The Lord hath made known his salvation: his righteousness hath he openly shewed in the sight of the heathen.

He hath remembered his mercy and his truth toward the house of Israel: all the ends of the earth have seen the salvation of our God.

Make a joyful noise unto the Lord, all the earth: make a loud noise, and rejoice, and sing praise.

Sing unto the Lord with the harp; with the harp, and the voice of a psalm.

With trumpets and sound of cornet make a joyful noise before the Lord, the King.

Let the sea roar, and the fulness thereof; the world, and they that dwell therein.

Let the floods clap their hands: let the hills be joyful together

Before the Lord; for he cometh to judge the earth: with righteousness shall he judge the world, and the people with equity.

LET US WITH A GLADSOME MIND

John Milton

Let us with a gladsome mind
Praise the Lord for He is kind;
For His mercies aye endure,
Ever faithful, ever sure.

Let us blaze His name abroad,
For of gods He is the God;
Who by all-commanding might,
Filled the new-made world with light.

He the golden tressed sun
Caused all day his course to run;
Th' horned moon to shine by night,
'Mid her spangled sisters bright.

He His chosen race did bless,
In the wasteful wilderness;
He hath, with a piteous eye,
Looked upon our misery.

All things living He doth feed.
His full hand supplies their need;
For His mercies aye endure,
Ever faithful, ever sure.

WISDOM CAN BE OBTAINED ONLY FROM GOD

Job, Chapter 28

Surely there is a vein for the silver, and a place for gold where they fine it.
Iron is taken out of the earth, and brass is molten out of the stone.
He setteth an end to darkness, and searcheth out all perfection,
The stones of darkness, and the shadow of death.
The flood breaketh out from the inhabitant;
Even the waters forgotten of the foot: they are dried up, they are gone away from men.
As for the earth, out of it cometh bread: and under it is turned up as it were fire.
The stones of it are the place of sapphires: and it hath dust of gold.
There is a path which no fowl knoweth, and which the vulture's eye hath not seen:
The lion's whelps have not trodden it, nor the fierce lion passed by it.
He putteth forth his hand upon the rock;
He overturneth the mountains by the roots.
He cutteth out rivers among the rocks; and his eye seeth every precious thing.
He bindeth the floods from overflowing; and the thing that is hid bringeth he forth to light.
But where shall wisdom be found?

And where is the place of understanding?
Man knoweth not the price thereof; neither is it found in the land of the living.
The depth saith, It is not in me: and the sea saith, It is not with me.
It cannot be gotten for gold, neither shall silver be weighed for the price thereof.
It cannot be valued with the gold of Ophir, with the precious onyx, or the sapphire.
The gold and the crystal cannot equal it,
And the exchange of it shall not be for jewels of fine gold.
No mention shall be made of coral, or of pearls
For the price of wisdom is above rubies.
The topaz of Ethiopia shall not equal it, neither shall it be valued with pure gold.
Whence then cometh wisdom? and where is the place of understanding?
Seeing it is hid from the eyes of all living, and kept close from the fowls of the air.
Destruction and death say, We have heard the fame thereof with our ears.
God understandeth the way thereof, and he knoweth the place thereof.
For he looketh to the ends of the earth, and seeth under the whole heaven;
To make the weight for the winds; and he weigheth the waters by measure.
When he made a decree for the rain, and a way for the lightning of the thunder:

Then did he see it, and declare it; he prepared it, yea,
and searched it out.
And unto man he said, Behold,
The fear of the Lord, that is wisdom; and to depart
from evil is understanding.

BY DOING GOOD WE LIVE

Josephine Troup

A CERTAIN wise man, deeply versed
In all the learning of the East,
Grew tired in spirit, and athirst
From life to be released.

So to Eliab, holy man
Of God he came: "Ah, give me, friend,
The herb of death, that now the span
Of my vain life may end."

Eliab gently answered: "Ere
The soul may free itself indeed,
This herb of healing thou must bear
To seven men in need;

"When thou hast lightened each man's grief,
And brought him hope and joy again,
Return; nor shalt thou seek relief
At Allah's hands in vain."

The wise man sighed, and humbly said:
"As Allah willeth, so is best."
And with the healing herb he sped
Away upon his quest.

And as he journeyed on, intent
To serve the sorrowing in the land
On deeds of love and mercy bent,
The herb bloomed in his hand,

And through his pulses shot a fire
Of strength and hope and happiness;
His heart leaped with a glad desire
To live and serve and bless.

Lord of all earthly woe and need,
Be this, life's flower, mine!
To love, to comfort, and to heal–
Therein is life divine!

HYMN

Martin Luther

Translated by FREDERICK HEDGE

A MIGHTY fortress is our God
  A bulwark never failing;
Our helper he amid the flood
  Of mortal ills prevailing.
    For still our ancient foe,
    Doth seek to work us woe;
    His craft and power are great,
    And, armed with cruel hate
  On earth has not his equal.

Did we in our own strength confide,
  Our striving would be losing,–
Were not the right man on our side,
  The man of God's own choosing.
    Dost ask who that may be?
    Christ Jesus, it is he,
    Lord Sabaoth is his name,
    From age to age the same,
  And he must win the battle.

And though this world, with devils filled,
  Should threaten to undo us,
We will not fear for God hath willed
  His truth to triumph through us.
    The Prince of darkness grim,
    We tremble not for him,

His rage we can endure,
For lo! his doom is sure,
One little word shall fell him.

That word above all earthly powers,
No thanks to them, abideth;
The spirit and the gifts are ours
Through Him who with us sideth.
Let goods and kindred go,
This mortal life also;
The body they may kill,
God's truth abideth still,
His kingdom is forever.

RAYER IN THE PROSPECT OF DEATH

Robert Burns

O Thou unknown, Almighty Cause
Of all my hope and fear!
In whose dread presence, ere an hour,
Perhaps I must appear!

If I have wander'd in those paths
Of life I ought to shun–
As something loudly in my breast,
Remonstrates I have done–

Thou know'st that Thou hast formèd me
With passions wild and strong;
And list'ning to their witching voice
Has often led me wrong.

Where human weakness has come short,
Or frailty stept aside,
Do Thóu, All-Good–for such Thou art–
In shades of darkness hide.

Where with intention I have err'd,
No other plea I have,
But, Thou art good; and Goodness still
Delighteth to forgive.

THE SOUL THAT DWELLS IN GOD SECURE FROM ALL EVIL

Psalm 91

HE THAT dwelleth in the secret place of the most High
Shall abide under the shadow of the Almighty.
I will say of the Lord, He is my refuge and my fortress: my God;
In Him will I trust.
Surely He shall deliver thee from the snare of the fowler, and from the noisome pestilence.
He shall cover thee with His feathers, and under His wings shalt thou trust.
His truth shall be thy shield and buckler.
Thou shalt not be afraid for the terror by night;
Nor for the arrow that flieth by day;
Nor for the pestilence that walketh in darkness;
Nor for the destruction that wasteth at noonday.
A thousand shall fall at thy side, and ten thousand at thy right hand;
But it shall not come nigh thee.
Only with thine eyes shalt thou behold and see the reward of the wicked.
Because thou hast made the Lord, which is my refuge, even the most High, thy habitation;
There shall no evil befall thee;
Neither shall any plague come nigh thy dwelling.
For he shall give his angels charge over thee, to keep thee in all thy ways.
They shall bear thee up in their hands, lest thou dash thy foot against a stone.

Thou shalt tread upon the lion and adder:
The young lion and the dragon shalt thou trample under feet.
Because he hath set his love upon me, therefore will I deliver him;
I will set him on high, because he hath known my name.
He shall call upon me, and I will answer him:
I will be with him in trouble;
I will deliver him, and honour him.
With long life will I satisfy him, and shew him my salvation.

THANATOPSIS

William Cullen Bryant

To HIM who in the love of Nature holds
Communion with her visible forms, she speaks
A various language; for his gayer hours
She has a voice of gladness, and a smile
And eloquence of beauty, and she glides
Into his darker musings, with a mild
And healing sympathy, that steals away
Their sharpness, ere he is aware. When thoughts
Of the last bitter hour come like a blight
Over thy spirit, and sad images
Of the stern agony, and shroud, and pall,
And breathless darkness, and the narrow house,
Make thee to shudder and grow sick at heart;–
Go forth, under the open sky, and list
To Nature's teachings, while from all around–
Earth and her waters, and the depths of air–
Comes a still voice:–

Yet a few days, and thee
The all-beholding sun shall see no more
In all his course; nor yet in the cold ground,
Where thy pale form was laid with many tears,
Nor in the embrace of ocean, shall exist
Thy image. Earth, that nourished thee, shall claim
Thy growth, to be resolved to earth again,
And, lost each human trace, surrendering up
Thine individual being, shalt thou go
To mix forever with the elements,

To be a brother to the insensible rock
And to the sluggish clod, which the rude swain
Turns with his share, and treads upon. The oak
Shall send his roots abroad, and pierce thy mould.

Yet not to thine eternal resting-place
Shalt thou retire alone, nor couldst thou wish
Couch more magnificent. Thou shalt lie down
With patriarchs of the infant world–with kings,
The powerful of the earth–the wise, the good,
Fair forms, and hoary seers of ages past,
All in one mighty sepulchre. The hills
Rock-ribbed and ancient as the sun,–the vales
Stretching in pensive quietness between;
The venerable woods–rivers that move
In majesty, and the complaining brooks
That make the meadows green; and, poured round all,
Old Ocean's gray and melancholy waste,–
Are but the solemn decorations all
Of the great tomb of man. The golden sun,
The planets, all the infinite host of heaven,
Are shining on the sad abodes of death
Through the still lapse of ages. All that tread
The globe are but a handful to the tribes
That slumber in its bosom.–Take the wings
Of morning, pierce the Barcan wilderness,
Or lose thyself in the continuous woods
Where rolls the Oregon, and hears no sound,
Save his own dashings–yet the dead are there;
And millions in those solitudes, since first
The flight of years began, have laid them down

In their last sleep–the dead reign there alone.
So shalt thou rest, and what if thou withdraw
In silence from the living, and no friend
Take note of thy departure? All that breathe
Will share thy destiny. The gay will laugh
When thou art gone, the solemn brood of care
Plod on, and each one as before will chase
His favourite phantom; yet all these shall leave
Their mirth and their employments, and shall come
And make their bed with thee. As the long train
Of ages glides away, the sons of men–
The youth in life's fresh spring, and he who goes
In the full strength of years, matron and maid,
The speechless babe, and the gray-headed man–
Shall one by one be gathered to thy side,
By those, who in their turn shall follow them.

So live, that when thy summons comes to join
The innumerable caravan, which moves
To that mysterious realm, where each shall take
His chamber in the silent halls of death,
Thou go not, like the quarry-slave at night,
Scourged to his dungeon, but, sustained and soothed
By an unfaltering trust, approach thy grave
Like one who wraps the drapery of his couch
About him, and lies down to pleasant dreams.

THE RIGHTEOUS AND THE WICKED CONTRASTED

Psalm 1

BLESSED is the man that walketh not in the counsel of the ungodly,
Nor standeth in the way of sinners, nor sitteth in the seat of the scornful.
But his delight is in the law of the Lord;
And in his law doth he meditate day and night.
And he shall be like a tree planted by the rivers of water, that bringeth forth his fruit in his season;
His leaf also shall not wither; and whatsoever he doeth shall prosper.
The ungodly are not so: but are like the chaff which the wind driveth away.
Therefore the ungodly shall not stand in the judgment,
Nor sinners in the congregation of the righteous.
For the Lord knoweth the way of the righteous: but the way of the ungodly shall perish.

O WHY SHOULD THE SPIRIT OF MORTAL BE PROUD?

William Knox

O WHY should the spirit of mortal be proud?
Like swift-flitting meteor, a fast-flying cloud,
A flash of the lightning, a break of the wave,
He passeth from life to his rest in the grave.

The leaves of the oak and the willow shall fade,
Be scattered around and together be laid;
And the young and the old, and the low and the high,
Shall moulder to dust and together shall lie.

The child that a mother attended and loved,
The mother that infant's affection who proved,
The husband that mother and infant who blessed,
Each, all, are away to their dwellings of rest.

The maid on whose brow, on whose cheek, in whose
eye,
Shone beauty and pleasure,–her triumphs are by;
And the memory of those who have loved her and
praised,
Are alike from the minds of the living erased.

The hand of the king that the sceptre hath borne,
The brow of the priest that the mitre hath worn,
The eyes of the sage, and the heart of the brave,–
Are hidden and lost in the depths of the grave.

The peasant whose lot was to sow and to reap,
The herdsman who climbed with his goats to the
steep,
The beggar who wandered in search of his bread,–
Have faded away like the grass that we tread.

The saint who enjoyed the communion of heaven,
The sinner who dared to remain unforgiven,
The wise and the foolish, the guilty and just,
Have quietly mingled their bones in the dust.

So the multitude goes, like the flower and the weed,
That wither away to let others succeed;
So the multitude comes, like those we behold,
To repeat every tale that hath often been told.

For we are the things our fathers have been;
We see the same sights that our fathers have seen,–
We drink the same stream, we feel the same sun,
And run the same course that our fathers have run.

The thoughts we are thinking our fathers would think;
From the death we are shrinking, they, too, would
shrink;
To the life we are clinging, they too would cling;
But it speeds from us all like the bird on the wing.

They loved, but their story we cannot unfold;
They scorned, but the heart of the haughty is cold;
They grieved, but no wail from their slumbers will
come;
They joyed, but the voice of their gladness is dumb.

They died,–ay, they died; and we things that are now,
Who walk on the turf that lies over their brow,
Who make in their dwellings a transient abode,
Meet the changes they met on their pilgrimage road.

Yea, hope and despondency, pleasure and pain,
Are mingled together in sunshine and rain;
And the smile and the tear, and the song and the dirge
Still follow each other like surge upon surge.

'Tis the wink of an eye, 'tis the draught of a breath,
From the blossom of health to the paleness of death,
From the gilded saloon to the bier and the shroud,–
Oh, why should the spirit of mortal be proud?

THE DESTRUCTION OF SENNACHERIB

Lord Byron

THE ASSYRIAN came down like the wolf on the fold,
And his cohorts were gleaming in purple and gold;
And the sheen of their spears was like stars on the sea,
When the blue wave rolls nightly on deep Galilee.

Like the leaves of the forest when summer is green,
That host with their banners at sunset were seen;
Like the leaves of the forest when autumn hath blown,
That host on the morrow lay withered and strown.

For the Angel of Death spread his wings on the blast,
And breathed in the face of the foe as he passed;
And the eyes of the sleepers waxed deadly and chill,
And their hearts but once heaved, and forever grew still!

And there lay the steed with his nostril all wide,
But through it there rolled not the breath of his pride:
And the foam of his gasping lay white on the turf,
And cold as the spray of the rock-beating surf.

And there lay the rider distorted and pale,
With the dew on his brow and the rust on his mail;
And the tents were all silent, the banners alone,
The lances unlifted, the trumpet unblown.

And the widows of Ashur are loud in their wail,
And the idols are broke in the temple of Baal;
And the might of the Gentile, unsmote by the sword,
Hath melted like snow in the glance of the Lord!

THE NAMELESS SAINTS

Edward Everett Hale

I

WHAT WAS his name? I do not know his name.
I only know he heard God's voice and came,
Brought all he had across the sea
To live and work for God and me;
Felled the ungracious oak;
Dragged from the soil
With horrid toil
The thrice-gnarled roots and stubborn rock;
With plenty piled the haggard mountain-side;
And at the end, without memorial, died.
No blaring trumpets sounded out his fame,
He lived,–he died,–I do not know his name.

II

No form of bronze and no memorial stones
Show me the place where lie his mouldering bones.
Only a cheerful city stands
Builded by his hardened hands.
Only ten thousand homes
Where every day
The cheerful play
Of love and hope and courage comes.
These are his monument, and these alone.
There is no form of bronze and no memorial stone.

III

And I?
Is there some desert or some pathless sea
Where Thou, Good God of angels, wilt send me?
  Some oak for me to rend; some sod,
    Some rock for me to break;
    Some handful of His corn to take
      And scatter far afield,
      Till it, in turn, shall yield
        Its hundredfold
        Of grains of gold
  To feed the waiting children of my God?
Show me the desert, Father, or the sea.
Is it Thine enterprise? Great God, send me.
And though this body lie where ocean rolls,
Count me among all Faithful Souls.

VESTIGIA

Bliss Carman

I TOOK a day to search for God,
And found Him not. But as I trod
  By rocky ledge, through woods untamed,
  Just where one scarlet lily flamed,
I saw His footprint in the sod.

Then suddenly, all unaware,
Far off in the deep shadows, where
  A solitary hermit thrush
  Sang through the holy twilight hush–
I heard His voice upon the air.

And even as I marveled how
God gives us Heaven here and now,
  In a stir of wind that hardly shook
  The poplar leaves beside the brook–
His hand was light upon my brow.

At last with evening as I turned
Homeward, and thought what I had learned
  And all that there was still to probe–
  I caught the glory of His robe
Where the last fires of sunset burned.

Back to the world with quickening start
I looked and longed for any part
  In making saving Beauty be . . .
  And from that kindling ecstasy
I knew God dwelt within my heart.

GOD IS THE ETERNAL REFUGE OF HIS PEOPLE

Psalm 46

God is our refuge and strength, a very present help in trouble.

Therefore will not we fear, though the earth be removed, and though the mountains be carried into the midst of the sea;

Though the waters thereof roar and be troubled, though the mountains shake with the swelling thereof. Selah.

There is a river, the streams whereof shall make glad the city of God, the holy place of the tabernacles of the most High.

God is in the midst of her; she shall not be moved: God shall help her, and that right early.

The heathen raged, the kingdoms were moved: he uttered his voice, the earth melted.

The Lord of hosts is with us; the God of Jacob is our refuge. Selah.

Come, behold the works of the Lord, what desolations he hath made in the earth.

He maketh wars to cease unto the end of the earth; he breaketh the bow, and cutteth the spear in sunder; he burneth the chariot in the fire.

Be still, and know that I am God: I will be exalted among the heathen, I will be exalted in the earth.

The Lord of hosts is with us; the God of Jacob is our refuge. Selah.

PARADISE

Christina Rossetti

ONCE IN a dream I saw the flowers
    That bud and bloom in Paradise;
    More fair are they than waking eyes
Have seen in all this world of ours.
And faint the perfume-bearing rose,
    And faint the lily on its stem,
And faint the perfect violet,
    Compared with them.

I heard the songs of Paradise;
    Each bird sat singing in its place;
    A tender song so full of grace
It soared like incense to the skies.
Each bird sat singing to its mate
    Soft cooing notes among the trees:
The nightingale herself were cold
    To such as these.

I saw the fourfold River flow,
    And deep it was, with golden sand;
    It flowed between a mossy land
With murmured music grave and low.
It hath refreshment for all thirst,
    For fainting spirits strength and rest:
Earth holds not such a draught as this
    From east to west.

The Tree of Life stood budding there,
Abundant with its twelvefold fruits;
Eternal sap sustains its roots,
Its shadowing branches fill the air.
Its leaves are healing for the world,
Its fruit the hungry world can feed
Sweeter than honey to the taste
And balm indeed.

I saw the Gate called Beautiful;
And looked, but scarce could look within;
I saw the golden streets begin,
And outskirts of the glassy pool.
Oh harps, oh crowns of plenteous stars,
Oh green palm-branches, many-leaved–
Eye hath not seen, nor ear hath heard,
Nor heart conceived.

I hope to see these things again,
But not as once in dreams by night;
To see them with my very sight,
And touch and handle and attain:
To have all heaven beneath my feet
For narrow way that once they trod;
To have my part with all the saints
And with my God.

THE LOVE OF GOD

Bernard Rascas

Translated by WILLIAM CULLEN BRYANT

ALL THINGS that are on earth shall wholly pass away,
Except the love of God, which shall live and last for aye.
The forms of men shall be as they had never been;
The blasted groves shall lose their fresh and tender green;
The birds of the thicket shall end their pleasant song,
And the nightingale shall cease to chant the evening long.
The kine of the pasture shall feel the dart that kills,
And all the fair white flocks shall perish from the hills.
The goat and antlered stag, the wolf and the fox,
The wild boar of the wood, and the chamois of the rocks,
And the strong and fearless bear, in the trodden dust shall lie;
And the dolphin of the sea, and the mighty whale, shall die.
And realms shall be dissolved, and empires be no more,
And they shall bow to death, who ruled from shore to shore;
And the great globe itself, so the Holy Writings tell,
With the rolling firmament, where the starry armies dwell,
Shall melt with fervent heat,–they shall all pass away,
Except the love of God, which shall live and last for aye!

EASILY GIVEN

It was only a sunny smile,
And little it cost in the giving;
But it scattered the night
Like morning light,
And made the day worth living.
Through life's dull warp a woof it wove,
In shining colors of light and love,
And the angels smiled as they watched above,
Yet little it cost in giving.

It was only a kindly word,
And a word that was lightly spoken;
Yet not in vain,
For it stilled the pain
Of a heart that was nearly broken.
It strengthened a fate beset by fears
And groping blindly through mists of tears
For light to brighten the coming years,
Although it was lightly spoken.

It was only a helping hand,
And it seemed of little availing;
But its clasps were warm,
And it saved from harm
A brother whose strength was failing.
Its touch was tender as angels' wings,
But it rolled the stone from the hidden springs,

And pointed the way to higher things,
  Though it seemed of little availing.

A smile, a word, a touch,
  And each is easily given;
    Yet one may win
    A soul from sin
  Or smooth the way to heaven.
A smile may lighten a falling heart,
A word may soften pain's keenest smart,
A touch may lead us from sin apart–
  How easily each is given!

THE IMAGE OF GOD

Francesco de Aldana

Translated by HENRY W. LONGFELLOW

O LORD! who seest from yon starry height,
Centred in one the future and the past,
Fashioned in thine own image, see how fast
The world obscures in me what once was bright!
Eternal sun! the warmth which thou hast given,
To cheer life's flowery April, fast decays;
Yet in the hoary winter of my days,
Forever green shall be my trust in heaven.
Celestial King! oh, let thy presence pass
Before my spirit, and an image fair
Shall meet that look of mercy from on high,
As the reflected image in a glass
Doth meet the look of him who seeks it there,
And owes its being to the gazer's eye.

THE UNIVERSAL PRAYER

Alexander Pope

FATHER OF all! In every age,
In every clime adored,
By saint, by savage, and by sage
Jehovah, Jove, or Lord!

Thou Great First Cause, least understood,
Who all my sense confined
To know but this, that thou art good,
And that myself am blind!

Yet gave me, in this dark estate,
To see the good from ill;
And, binding nature fast in fate,
Left free the human will.

What conscience dictates to be done,
Or warns me not to do,
This teach me more than hell to shun,
That more than heaven pursue.

What blessings thy free bounty gives,
Let me not cast away;
For God is paid when man receives;
To enjoy is to obey.

Yet not to earth's contracted span
Thy goodness let me bound,
Or think thee Lord alone of man,
When thousand worlds are round.

Let not this weak, unknowing hand
Presume thy bolts to throw,
And deal damnation round the land
On each I judge thy foe.

If I am right, thy grace impart
Still in the right to stay;
If I am wrong, Oh, teach my heart
To find the better way!

Save me alike from foolish pride,
And impious discontent,
At aught thy wisdom has denied,
Or aught thy goodness lent.

Teach me to feel another's woe,
To hide the fault I see;
That mercy I to others show,
That mercy show to me.

Mean though I am, not wholly so,
Since quickened by thy breath;
Oh, lead me wheresoe'er I go,
Through this day's life or death.

This day be bread and peace my lot;
All else beneath the sun
Thou knowest if best bestowed or not,
And let thy will be done.

To thee, whose temple is all space,–
  Whose altar, earth, sea, skies,–
One chorus let all beings raise!
  All Nature's incense rise!

THE EXILE LONGS FOR THE HOUSE OF GOD

Psalm 42

As THE hart panteth after the water brooks,
So panteth my soul after thee, O God.
My soul thirsteth for God, for the living God:
When shall I come and appear before God?
My tears have been my meat day and night,
While they continually say unto me, Where is thy God?
When I remember these things, I pour out my soul in me;
For I had gone with the multitude,
I went with them to the house of God, with the voice of joy and praise, with a multitude that kept holyday.
Why art thou cast down, O my soul? and why art thou disquieted in me?
Hope thou in God: for I shall yet praise him for the help of his countenance.
O my God, my soul is cast down within me:
Therefore will I remember thee from the land of Jordan,
And of the Hermonites, from the hill Mizar.
Deep calleth unto deep at the noise of thy waterspouts;
All thy waves and thy billows are gone over me.
Yet the Lord will command his lovingkindness in the daytime,
And in the night his song shall be with me, and my prayer unto the God of my life.

I will say unto God my rock, Why hast thou forgotten me?
Why go I mourning because of the oppression of the enemy?
As with a sword in my bones, mine enemies reproach me;
While they say daily unto me, Where is thy God?
Why art thou cast down, O my soul?
And why art thou disquieted within me?
Hope thou in God: for I shall yet praise him, who is the health of my countenance, and my God.

COMMUNION

John B. Tabb

ONCE WHEN my heart was passion free
To learn of things divine,
The soul of nature suddenly
Outpoured itself in mine.

I held the secrets of the deep
And of the heavens above;
I knew the harmonies of sleep,
The mysteries of love.

And for a moment's interval
The earth, the sky, the sea–
My soul encompassed each and all,
As now they encompass me.

To one in all, to all in one–
Since love the work began
Life's everwidening circles run
Revealing God to man.

A THANKSGIVING TO GOD

Robert Herrick

LORD, THOU hast given me a cell
  Wherein to dwell;
A little house, whose humble roof
  Is weather-proof;
Under the sparres of which I lie,
  Both soft and drie;
Where thou, my chamber for to ward,
  Hast set a guard
Of harmless thoughts, to watch and keep
  Me while I sleep.
Low is my porch, as is my Fate,
  Both void of state;
And yet the threshold of my door,
  Is worn by the poore,
Who hither come and freely get
  Good words, or meat:
Like as my parlour, so my hall
  And kitchen's small;
A little butterie, and therein
  A little bin,
Which keeps my little loaf of bread
  Unchipt, unflead:
Some brittle sticks of thorn and brier
  Make me a fire,
Close by whose loving coals I sit,
  And glow like it.
Lord I confess, too, when I dine
  The pulse is thine,

And all those other bits that bee
  There placed by Thee;
The worts, the purslane and the messe
  Of watercresse,
Which of thy kindness thou hast sent;
  And my content
Makes those and my belovèd beet
  To be more sweet.
'Tis Thou that crownst my glittering hearth
  With guiltless mirth;
And giv'st me wassaile bowles to drink,
  Spiced to the brink.
Lord 'tis Thy plenty-dropping hand
  That soiles my land,
And giv'st me for my bushel sowne
  Twice ten for one:
Thou mak'st my teeming hen to lay
  Her egg each day;
Beside my healthful ewes to bear
  Me twins each yeare;
The while the conduits of my kine
  Run creame for wine.

All these and better thou dost send
  Me to this end,–
That I should render, for my part,
  A thankful heart;
Which, fired with incense, I resigne
  As wholly Thine;
But the acceptance, that must be,
  My Christ, by thee.

LIGHT SHINING OUT OF DARKNESS

William Cowper

GOD MOVES in a mysterious way
His wonders to perform;
He plants his footsteps in the sea,
And rides upon the storm.

Deep in unfathomable mines
Of never-failing skill
He treasures up his bright designs,
And works his sovereign will.

Ye fearful saints, fresh courage take,
The clouds ye so much dread
Are big with mercy, and shall break
In blessings on your head.

Judge not the Lord by feeble sense,
But trust him for his grace:
Behind a frowning providence
He hides a smiling face.

His purposes will ripen fast,
Unfolding every hour;
The bud may have a bitter taste
But sweet will be the flower.

Blind unbelief is sure to err,
And scan his work in vain;
God is his own interpreter
And he will make it plain.

THE KING OF GLORY ENTERING ZION

Psalm 24

THE EARTH is the Lord's, and the fulness thereof;
The world, and they that dwell therein.
For he hath founded it upon the seas, and established it upon the floods.
Who shall ascend into the hill of the Lord?
Or who shall stand in his holy place?
He that hath clean hands, and a pure heart;
Who hath not lifted up his soul unto vanity, nor sworn deceitfully.
He shall receive the blessing from the Lord, and righteousness from the God of his salvation.
This is the generation of them that seek him, that seek thy face, O Jacob.
Selah.
Lift up your heads, O ye gates; and be ye lift up, ye everlasting doors;
And the King of glory shall come in.
Who is this King of glory? The Lord strong and mighty,
The Lord mighty in battle.
Lift up your heads, O ye gates;
Even lift them up, ye everlasting doors; and the King of glory shall come in.
Who is this King of glory?
The Lord of hosts, he is the King of glory.
Selah.

A STRIP OF BLUE

Lucy Larcom

I DO NOT OWN an inch of land,
But all I see is mine,–
The orchards and the mowing-fields,
The lawns and gardens fine.
The winds my tax collectors are,
They bring me tithes divine,–
Wild scents and subtle essences,
A tribute rare and free;
And, more magnificent than all,
My window keeps for me
A glimpse of blue immensity,–
A little strip of sea.

Richer am I than he who owns
Great fleets and argosies;
I have a share in every ship
Won by the inland breeze,
To loiter on yon airy road
Above the apple trees.
I freight them with my untold dreams;
Each bears my own picked crew;
And nobler cargoes wait for them
Than ever India knew,–
My ships that sail into the East
Across that outlet blue.

Sometimes they seem like living shapes,–
The people of the sky,–

Guests in white raiment coming down
  From heaven, which is close by;
I call them by familiar names,
  As one by one draws nigh,
So white, so light, so spirit-like
  From violet mists they bloom!
The aching wastes of the unknown
  Are half reclaimed from gloom,
Since on life's hospitable sea
  All souls find sailing room.

The ocean grows a weariness
  With nothing else in sight;
Its east and west, its north and south,
  Spread out from morn to night;
We miss the warm, caressing shore,
  Its brooding shade and light.
A part is greater than the whole;
  By hints are mysteries told.
The fringes of eternity,–
  God's sweeping garment-fold,
In that bright shred of glittering sea,
  I reach out for, and hold.

The sails, like flakes of roseate pearl,
  Float in upon the mist;
The waves are broken precious stones,–
  Sapphire and amethyst,
Washed from celestial basement walls,
  By suns unsetting kissed.
Out through the utmost gates of space,

Past where the grey stars drift,
To the widening Infinite, my soul
Glides on, a vessel swift,
Yet loses not her anchorage
In yonder azure rift.

Here I sit as a little child
The threshold of God's door
Is that clear band of chrysoprase;
Now the vast temple floor,
The blinding glory of the dome
I bow my head before.
Thy universe, O God, is home,
In height or depth, to me;
Yet here upon thy footstool green
Content I am to be.
Glad, when is opened unto my need
Some sea-like glimpse of thee.

GOD MAKES A PATH

Roger Williams

GOD MAKES a path, provides a guide,
  And feeds a wilderness;
His glorious name, while breath remains,
  O that I may confess.

Lost many a time, I have had no guide,
  No house but a hollow tree!
In stormy winter night no fire,
  No food, no company;

In Him I found a house, a bed,
  A table, company;
No cup so bitter but's made sweet,
  Where God shall sweetening be.

FAITH

George Santayana

O WORLD, thou choosest not the better part!
It is not wisdom to be only wise,
And on the inward vision close the eyes,
But it is wisdom to believe the heart.
Columbus found a world and had no chart,
Save one that faith deciphered in the skies;
To trust the soul's invincible surmise
Was all his science and his only art.
Our knowledge is a torch of smoky pine
That lights the pathway but one step ahead
Across a void of mystery and dread.
Bid, then, the tender light of faith to shine
By which alone the mortal heart is led
Unto the thinking of the thought divine.

AN INVOCATION

John Addington Symonds

To God, the everlasting, who abides,
One Life within things infinite that die:
To Him whose purity no thought divides:
Whose breath is breathed through immensity.

Him neither eye hath seen, nor ear hath heard;
Yet reason, seated in the souls of men,
Though, pondering oft on the mysterious word,
Hath e'er revealed His Being to mortal ken.

Earth changes, and the starry wheels roll round;
The seasons come and go, moons wax and wane;
The nations rise and fall, and fill the ground,
Storing the sure results of joy and pain:

Slow knowledge widens toward a perfect whole,
From that first man who named the heaven,
To Him who weighs the planets as they roll,
And knows what laws to every life are given.

Yet He appears not. Round the extreme sphere
Of science still thin ether floats unseen:
Darkness still wraps Him round; and ignorant fear
Remains of what we are, and what have been.

Only we feel Him; in aching dreams,
Swift intuitions, pangs of keen delight,
The sudden vision of His glory seems
To sear our souls, dividing the dull night:

And we yearn toward Him. Beauty, Goodness, Truth;
These three are one; one life, one thought, one being;
One source of still rejuvenescent youth;
One light for endless and unclouded seeing.

Mere symbols we perceive–the dying beauty,
The partial truth that few can comprehend,
The vacillating faith, the painful duty,
The virtue laboring to a dubious end.

O God, unknown, invisible, secure,
Whose being by dim resemblances we guess,
Who in man's fear and love abidest sure,
Whose power we feel in darkness and confess!

Without Thee nothing is, and Thou art nought
When on Thy substance we gaze curiously:
By Thee impalpable, named Force and Thought,
The solid world ceases not to be.

THE HEAVENS ABOVE AND THE LAW WITHIN

Psalm 19

THE HEAVENS declare the glory of God;
And the firmament sheweth his handiwork.
Day unto day uttereth speech,
And night unto night sheweth knowledge.
There is no speech nor language, where their voice is not heard.
Their line is gone out through all the earth, and their words to the end of the world.
In them hath he set a tabernacle for the sun,
Which is as a bridegroom coming out of his chamber,
And rejoiceth as a strong man to run a race.
His going forth is from the end of the heaven, and his circuit unto the ends of it;
And there is nothing hid from the heat thereof.
The law of the Lord is perfect, converting the soul;
The testimony of the Lord is sure, making wise the simple.
The statutes of the Lord are right, rejoicing the heart;
The commandment of the Lord is pure, enlightening the eyes.
The fear of the Lord is clean, enduring for ever;
The judgments of the Lord are true and righteous altogether.
More to be desired are they than gold, yea, than much fine gold;
Sweeter also than honey and the honeycomb.
Moreover by them is thy servant warned;

And in keeping of them there is great reward.
Who can understand his errors? Cleanse thou me from
secret faults.
Keep back thy servant also from presumptuous sins;
let them not have dominion over me;
Then shall I be upright, and I shall be innocent from
the great transgression.
Let the words of my mouth, and the meditation of
my heart, be acceptable in thy sight,
O Lord, my strength, and my redeemer.

Song from PIPPA PASSES

Robert Browning

THE year's at the spring
The day's at the morn;
Morning's at seven;
The hillside's dew-pearled;
The lark's on the wing;
The snail's on the thorn;
God's in his heaven–
All's right with the world.

SALUTATION TO JESUS CHRIST

John Calvin

I GREET thee, my Redeemer sure,
  I trust in none but thee,
Thou who hast borne such toil and shame
  And suffering for me:
Our hearts from cares and cravings vain
  And foolish fears set free.

Thou art the King compassionate,
  Thou reignest everywhere,
Almighty Lord, reign thou in us,
  Rule all we have and are:
Enlighten us and raise to heaven,
  Amid thy glories there.

Thou art the life by which we live;
  Our stay and strength's in thee;
Uphold us so in face of death,
  What time soe'er it be,
That we may meet it with strong heart,
  And may die peacefully.

The true and perfect gentleness
  We find in thee alone;
Make us to know thy loveliness,
  Teach us to love thee known;
Grant us sweet fellowship with thee,
  And all who are thine own.

Our hope is in none else but thee;
  Faith holds thy promise fast;
Be pleased, Lord, to strengthen us,
  Whom Thou redeemed hast,
To bear all troubles patiently,
  And overcome at last.

Children of Eve and heirs of ill,
  To thee thy banished cry;
To thee in sorrow's vale we bring
  Our sighs and misery;
We take the sinners' place and plead:
  Lord, save us, or we die.

Look Thou, our Daysman and High Priest
  Upon our low estate;
Make us to see God's face in peace
  Through thee, our Advocate;
With thee, our Savior, may our feet
  Enter at heaven's gate.

Lord Jesus Christ of holy souls,
  The Bridegroom sweet and true,
Meet thou the rage of Anti-Christ,
  Break thou his nets in two;
Grant us thy Spirit's help, thy will
  In every deed to do.

SOME KEEP SUNDAY GOING TO CHURCH

Emily Dickinson

SOME KEEP Sunday going to church
  I keep it staying at home,
With a bobolink for a chorister,
  And an orchard for a throne.

Some keep Sabbath in surplice,
  I just wear my wings
And instead of tolling the bell for church,
  Our little sexton sings.

God preaches, a noted clergyman,
  And the sermon is never long,
So instead of going to heaven at last
  I'm going all along.

PSALM 8

Man's Place in Creation

O LORD our Lord, how excellent is thy name in all the earth!
Who hast set thy glory above the heavens.
Out of the mouth of babes and sucklings hast thou ordained strength because of thine enemies,
That thou mightest still the enemy and the avenger.
When I consider thy heavens, the work of thy fingers, the moon and the stars, which thou hast ordained;
What is man, that thou art mindful of him?
And the son of man, that thou visitest him?
For thou hast made him a little lower than the angels,
And hast crowned him with glory and honour.
Thou madest him to have dominion over the works of thy hands;
Thou hast put all things under his feet:
All sheep and oxen, yea, and the beasts of the field;
The fowl of the air, and the fish of the sea,
And whatsoever passeth through the paths of the seas.
O Lord our Lord,
How excellent is thy name in all the earth!

THE HOUND OF HEAVEN

Francis Thompson

I FLED Him, down the nights and down the days;
I fled Him down the arches of the years;
I fled Him down the labyrinthine ways
Of my own mind; and in the midst of tears
I hid from Him and under running laughter.
Up vistaed hopes I sped;
And shot, precipitated
Adown titanic glooms of chasmèd fears,
From those strong Feet that followed, followed after,
But with unhurrying chase
And unperturbèd pace,
Deliberate speed, majestic instancy
They beat–and a Voice beat
More instant than the Feet–
"All things betray thee, who betrayest Me."

I pleaded, outlaw-wise,
By many a hearted casement, curtained red,
Trellised with intertwining charities;
(For, though I knew His love Who followèd,
Yet I was sore adread
Lest having Him I must have naught beside;)
But, if one little casement parted wide,
The gust of His approach would clash it to.
Fear wist not to evade as Love wist to pursue.
Across the margent of the world I fled,
And troubled the gold gateways of the stars,

Smiting for shelter on their clangèd bars;
Fretted to dulcet jars
And silvern chatter the pale ports o' the moon.
I said to dawn, Be sudden; to eve, Be soon;
With thy young skyey blossoms heap me over
From this tremendous Lover!
Float thy vague veil about me, lest He see!
I tempted all His servitors, but to find
My own betrayal in their constancy,
In faith to Him their fickleness to me,
Their traitorous trueness, and their loyal deceit.
To all swift things for swiftness did I sue;
Clung to the whistling mane of every wind.
But whether they swept, smoothly fleet,
The long savannahs of the blue;
Or, whether, thunder-driven,
They clanged His chariot 'thwart a heaven
Plashy with flying lightnings round the spurn o' their feet;–
Fear wist not to evade as Love wist to pursue.
Still with unhurrying chase
And unperturbèd pace,
Deliberate speed, majestic instancy,
Came on the following Feet,
And a Voice above their beat–
"Naught shelters thee, who wilt not shelter Me."

I sought no more that after which I strayed,
In face of man or maid;
But still within the little children's eyes
Seems something, something that replies;

They are at least for me, surely for me!
I turned me to them very wistfully;
But just as their young eyes grew sudden fair
With dawning answers there,
Their angel plucked them from me by the hair.
"Come, then, ye other children–Nature's–share
With me" (said I) "your delicate fellowship;
Let me greet you, lip to lip,
Let me twine you with caresses,
Wantoning
With our Lady Mother's vagrant tresses,
Banqueting
With her in her wind-walled palace,
Underneath her azure dais.
Quaffing, as your taintless way is,
From a chalice
Lucent-weeping out of the dayspring."
So it was done:
I in their delicate fellowship was one–
Drew the bolt of nature's secrecies.
I knew all the swift importings
Of the wilful face of the skies,
I knew how the clouds arise
Spumèd of the wild sea snortings;
All that's born or dies
Rose and drooped with–made them shapers
Of mine own moods, or wailful or Divine–
With them joyed or was bereaven.
I was heavy with the even
When she lit her glimmering tapers
Round the day's dead sanctities.

I laughed in the morning's eyes.
I triumphed and I saddened with all weather,
Heaven and I wept together,
And its sweet tears were salt with mortal mine;
Against the red throb of its sunset-heart
I laid my own to beat,
And share commingling heat;
But not by that, by that, was eased my human smart.
In vain my tears were wet on Heaven's grey cheek.
For ah! we know not what each other says,
These things and I; in sound *I* speak–
Their sound is but their stir, they speak by silences.
Nature, poor stepdame, cannot slake my drouth;
Let her, if she would owe me,
Drop yon blue bosom-veil of sky, and show me
The breasts o' her tenderness:
Never did any milk of hers once bless
My thirsting mouth.
Nigh and nigh draws the chase
With unperturbèd pace,
Deliberate speed, majestic instancy;
And past those noisèd Feet
A voice comes yet more fleet–
"Lo, naught contents thee, who content'st not Me."

Naked I wait thy love's uplifted stroke.
My harness, piece by piece, thou hast hewn from me,
And smitten me to my knee;
I am defenseless utterly.
I slept, methinks, and woke
And slowly gazing, find me stripped in sleep.

In the rash lustihood of my young powers,
I stood the pillaring hours
And pulled my life upon me; grimed with smears
I stand amid the dust o' the mounded years–
My mangled youth lies dead beneath the heap.
My days have crackled and gone up in smoke,
Have puffed and burst as sun-starts on a stream.
Yea, faileth now even dream
The dreamer, and the lute the lutanist;
Even the linked fantasies in whose blossomy twist
I swung the earth, a trinket at my wrist,
Are yielding; cords of all too weak account
For earth with heavy griefs so overplussed.
Ah! is Thy love indeed
A weed, albeit an amaranthine weed,
Suffering no flowers except its own to mount?
Ah! must–
Designer Infinite!–
Ah, must Thou char the wood ere Thou canst limn
with it?
My freshness spent its wavering shower i' the dust:
And now my heart is as a broken fount,
Wherein tear-drippings stagnate, spilt down ever
From the dank thoughts that shiver
Upon the sighful branches of my mind.
Such is; what is to be?
The pulp so bitter, how shall taste the rind?
I dimly guess what Time in mists confounds:
Yet ever and anon a trumpet sounds
From the hid battlements of Eternity;
Those shaken mists a space unsettle, then

Round the half-glimpsèd turrets slowly wash again.
But not ere him who summoneth
I first have seen, enwound
With glooming robes purpureal, cypress-crowned;
His name I know and what his trumpet saith.
Whether man's heart or life it be which yields
Thee harvest, must Thy harvest fields
Be dunged with rotten death?

Now of that long pursuit
Comes on at hand the bruit;
That Voice is round me like a bursting sea:
"And is thy earth so marred,
Shattered in shard on shard?
Lo, all things fly thee, for thou flyest Me!
Strange, piteous, futile thing,
Wherefore should any set thee love apart?
Seeing none but I makes much of naught" (He said);
"And human love needs human meriting:
How hast thou merited—
Of all man's clotted clay the dingiest clot?
Alack, thou knowest not
How little worthy of any love thou art!
Whom wilt thou find to love ignoble thee
Save Me, save only Me?
All which I took from thee, I did but take
Not for thy harms,
But just that thou mightst seek it in My arms.
All which thy child's mistake
Fancies as lost, I have stored for thee at home:
Rise, clasp My hand and come!"

by me that footfall:
gloom, after all,
His hand, outstretched caressingly?
"Ah, fondest, blindest, weakest,
I am He Whom thou seekest!
Thou dravest love from thee, who dravest Me."

OUT IN THE FIELDS WITH GOD

Louise Imogen Guiney

THE LITTLE cares that fretted me
I lost them yesterday,
Among the fields above the sea,
Among the winds at play,
Among the lowing of the herds,
The rustling of the trees,
Among the singing of the birds,
The humming of the bees.

The foolish fears of what might happen,
I cast them all away
Among the clover-scented grass,
Among the new-mown hay,
Among the husking of the corn,
Where drowsy poppies nod
Where ill thoughts die and good are born—
Out in the fields with God.

THE LAMB

William Blake

Little lamb, who made thee?
Dost thou know who made thee?
Gave thee life and bade thee feed
By the stream and o'er the mead;
Gave thee clothing of delight,
Softest clothing, woolly, bright;
Gave thee such a tender voice,
Making all the vales rejoice?
Little lamb, who made thee?
Dost thou know who made thee?

Little lamb, I'll tell thee;
Little lamb, I'll tell thee;
He is callèd by thy name,
For he calls himself a lamb.
He is meek and he is mild,
He became a little child,–
I a child and thou a lamb,
We are callèd by his name.
Little lamb, God bless thee!
Little lamb, God bless thee!

CHARTLESS

Emily Dickinson

I NEVER saw a moor,
  I never saw the sea;
Yet know I how the heather looks,
  And what a wave must be.

I never talked with God,
  Nor visited in heaven;
Yet certain am I of the spot
  As if the chart were given.

MY CREED

Alice Cary

I HOLD THAT Christian grace abounds
Where charity is seen; that when
We climb to heaven, 'tis on the rounds
Of love to men.

I hold all else named piety
A selfish scheme, a vain pretense;
Where center is not—can there be
Circumference?

This I moreover hold, and dare
Affirm where'er my rhyme may go,—
Whatever things be sweet and fair,
Love makes them so.

Whether it be the lullabies
That charm to rest the nursling bird,
Or the sweet confidence of sighs
And blushes, made without a word.

Whether the dazzling and the flush
Of softly sumptuous garden bowers,
Or by some cabin door, a bush
Of ragged flowers.

'Tis not the wide phylactery,
Nor stubborn fast, nor stated prayers,

That make us saints: we judge the tree
  By what it bears.

And when a man can live apart
  From works, on theologic trust,
I know the blood about his heart
  Is dry as dust.

A PRAYER

William Dean Howells

LORD, FOR the erring thought
Not into evil wrought;
Lord, for the wicked will,
Betrayed and baffled still;
For the heart from itself kept,
Our thanksgiving accept!
For ignorant hopes that were
Broken at our blind prayer;
For pain, death, sorrow sent,
Unto our chastisement;
For all loss of seeming good,
Quicken our gratitude!

THE CHRISTIAN PILGRIM'S HYMN

William Williams

GUIDE ME, O thou great Jehovah,
Pilgrim through this barren land:
I am weak but thou art mighty;
Hold me with thy powerful hand:
Bread of heaven! Bread of heaven!
Feed me now and evermore!

Open now the crystal fountain
Whence the healing streams do flow;
Let the fiery cloudy pillar
Lead me all my journey through:
Strong Deliverer! Strong Deliverer!
Be thou still my strength and shield.

When I tread the verge of Jordan,
Bid my anxious fears subside;
Death of deaths, and hell's destruction,
Land me safe on Canaan's side:
Songs of praises, songs of praises,
I will ever give to thee.

Musing on my habitation,
Musing on my heavenly home,
Fills my soul with holy longing;
Come, my Jesus, quickly come!
Vanity is all I see;
Lord, I long to be with thee!

MY FAITH LOOKS UP TO THEE

Ray Palmer

My faith looks up to Thee,
Thou Lamb of Calvary,
Savior Divine;
Now hear me while I pray;
Take all my guilt away;
O, let me from this day
Be wholly Thine!

May Thy rich grace impart
Strength to my fainting heart,
My zeal inspire;
As thou hast died for me,
O, may my love to Thee
Pure, warm and changeless be,
A living fire!

While life's dark maze I tread,
And griefs around me spread,
Be thou my guide;
Bid darkness turn to day,
Wipe sorrow's tears away,
Nor let me ever stray
From Thee aside.

When ends life's transient dream,
When death's cold sullen stream
Shall o'er me roll;

Blest Savior then, in love,
Fear and distrust remove;
O, bear me safe above,
A ransomed soul!

THE DAY IS DYING IN THE WEST

Mary A. Lathbury

Day is dying in the west;
Heaven is touching earth with rest;
Wait and worship while the night
Sets the evening lamps alight,
  Through all the sky.

Refrain

Holy, holy, holy, Lord God of hosts!
Heaven and earth are full of Thee;
Heaven and earth are praising Thee,
  O Lord most high!

Lord of life, beneath the dome
Of the universe, Thy home,
Gather us, who seek Thy face
To the fold of Thy embrace,
  For Thou art nigh.

While the deepening shadows fall,
Heart of love, enfolding all,
Through the glory and the grace
Of the stars that veil Thy face,
  Our hearts ascend.

When forever from our sight
Pass the stars the day, the night,
Lord of Angels, on our eyes,
Let eternal morning rise,
  And shadows end.

INDEX OF AUTHORS

INDEX OF TITLES